PEACE

THROUGH EVERY

PROBLEM

BY CHAD MEZA

Peace Through Every Problem

ISBN: 978-1-387-90318-4

DEDICATION

To my dad, Dean Meza. You've inspired me to do things I never dreamed were possible. I'm proud to be your son.

CONTENTS

INTRODUCTION

We all deal with problems. And if we're honest about it, it's so easy to respond to these problems with fear, anxiety, shame, guilt, loneliness, depression, hopelessness, and a whole bunch of other nasty feelings. But what if I were to tell you that you don't have to respond like that? What if I were to tell you that you can experience peace no matter what kind of problem you're facing? "Really? No matter what kind of problem?" Yes, even when we're going through the toughest times in our lives, we can experience incredible peace.

Over the course of this book, I am going to tell you exactly how you can have peace through every problem. We are going to look at four simple truths that will not only help us experience peace, but radically transform the way we respond to problems in our lives. You'll never react to problems the same way again.

GOD CAN DO ANYTHING

What is your first instinct when you hear bad news? What's the first thing you do? What is the first thing you think about?

When my wife, Cynthia, was pregnant with our first child, she had a lot of complications. One night, when she was about seven months pregnant, she started having trouble breathing. So, I rushed her to the hospital. After some tests, the doctors gave us a rundown of all kinds of issues Cynthia was having. In a moment, the whole mood shifted, and the doctors began to move with an urgency. Basically, they told us that they needed to do an emergency C-section immediately. Cynthia was dying. As they are prepping Cynthia for the operation, they made it very clear that there was about a 90% chance that Cynthia was not going to make it through

3

the operation. To top it off, they said there was virtually no chance they would be able to save the baby.

I wish I could say that my first instinct was to trust God. I wish I could say that my first instinct was to pray. I wish I could say that my first instinct was to believe God for a miracle. But, if I'm honest, my initial response was fear, anxiety, worry, and stress.

I know I'm not the only one who has faced these kinds of problems. We all deal with hard times. We all deal with difficult circumstances.

Maybe you're dealing with something right now:

- Maybe you're having issues at work.

- Maybe you've lost your job.

- Maybe you're having financial difficulties, and don't know how you're going to get by.

- Maybe you're sick, or you're having some sort of health problem.

- Maybe your doctor has given you a bad report.

- Maybe you're in the middle of relationship problems.

- Maybe your marriage is falling apart.

It can be scary to go through these kinds of things. It can be scary not knowing how you're going to pay your rent. It can be scary to be diagnosed with a life-threatening disease. These things can be scary. These things can be stressful.

I've been there. I've been without a job. I've been without a home. I've been in times where it seemed like my marriage was falling apart. I've lost loved ones. And I'm just talking about my years as a Christian.

Problems are going to arise. Hard times are going strike. In fact, there might even be times we come face-to-face with situations that just seem impossible. The question is not whether or not we're going to face problems. The question is, how are we going to respond to them?

The tendency for many of us is to get all worked up over our problems. We get filled with fear. We get all worried and stressed out. When a tough circumstance comes our way, we tend to get so overwhelmed. It's like we get tunnel vision, where all we can see is this one thing, this one problem, this one situation. And all we can think about is:

- "What am I going to do?"

- "What's going to happen?"

- "What about this?"

- "What about that?"

It's like our whole world hinges on this one thing that is happening in our lives. Maybe you've been there.

I want to tell you something: we don't have to live like that, ever. We can have hope, joy, and peace, even when things are tough. But, how do we do that? The Bible teaches us a truth about God that can help us as we face problems that would normally cause us to be filled with fear and anxiety.

GENESIS 1:1

We're going to look at a short passage found at the very beginning of the Bible, Genesis 1:1. Let's read it:

> [1] In the beginning, God created the heavens and the earth.
>
> Genesis 1:1 (ESV)

In the beginning. When? In the beginning. Before anything. Before everything.

- Before there were 4K TVs.

- Before there were iPhones.

- Before the Internet.

- Before there were airplanes.

- Before there were cars.

- Before there were people.

- Before the Earth was created.

- Before there was time, matter, and space.

Before all that, God existed. This God who existed before all things is the one who created the entire universe. In fact, He created the universe out of nothing. The Bible says He created it by simply speaking it into existence.

> ⁶ The Lord merely spoke,
>   and the heavens were created.
> He breathed the word,
>   and all the stars were born.
> ⁷ He assigned the sea its boundaries
>   and locked the oceans in vast reservoirs.
> ⁸ Let the whole world fear the Lord,
>   and let everyone stand in awe of him.
> ⁹ For when he spoke, the world began!
>   It appeared at his command.

Psalm 33:6-9 (NLT)

Wow! How big is God if He can do that? How powerful is God if He can do that?

Think about how big Earth is. Think about the mountains and the oceans. Think about all the beautiful landscapes. God created all of that.

God created it out of nothing. He just spoke it into existence.

The most amazing part is that God didn't just create Earth, He created the whole universe. As big as Earth is, it is tiny compared to the rest of the universe.

Take the sun for example. Some people have suggested that over 1,000,000 Earths could fit inside the sun. Isn't that fascinating? We often see the sun as just a small circle in the sky that provides light, but in reality, it is a star that is bigger than our planet. And if you've ever looked up at a clear night sky, you've noticed there's more than one star in the universe. There are billions of these things in the universe. Not just hundreds, not just thousands, not just millions. But billions! The sun is just one of billions of stars. The Bible says that God spoke all of them into existence. What a mighty God! What a powerful God!

When you look at God's power through the creation of Earth and all that is in it, that's enough to paint a big picture of God. That's enough to showcase God's power, strength, and might. However, when you take into consideration the creation of the rest of the universe, it just magnifies that immensely.

I used to have a co-worker who was really into astronomy. In fact, he had even built his own telescope. One night, he invited my family to do some stargazing and try out his telescope. That night, he showed us the Andromeda galaxy. He then went on to explain that this galaxy is over 2,000,000 light-years away. That means that if we shined a light from the Andromeda galaxy, it would take over 2,000,000 years for that light to be seen on Earth. In other words, what we were seeing that night was Andromeda from about 2,000,000 years ago. To top it all off, Andromeda is just one of the billions of galaxies in our universe. Our God spoke all this into existence. How big is God if He can speak such a huge universe into existence?

For God to speak all things into existence, what does that say about Him? What does it say about His greatness? What does it say about His power? What does it say about His ability? I think it screams that God can do anything.

GOD CAN DO ANYTHING

God can do anything. If He can speak this gigantic universe into existence, there's absolutely nothing that He cannot do.

Honestly, think about it. In light of God's ability to speak all things into existence, is He not able to help us with our problems? Is He not able to help us with our financial issues, or our marital problems?

> [27] "I am the Lord, the God of all mankind. Is anything too hard for me?
>
> Jeremiah 32:27 (NIV)

When problems arise, when we're hit with hard times, when we're going through the fire, we can have faith that God can do anything. We can trust that God can do anything. God can make a difference. God can help us through. God can do a miracle.

No matter what comes against us, God is always bigger. God is bigger than our circumstances. God is bigger than our problems.

The Bible records a situation in 1 Samuel 17, where an army had come to fight against Israel. This opposing army had a soldier named Goliath. Goliath was a giant, and he was taunting the army of Israel, challenging anyone to a one-on-one fight. Then a young teenager, David, decides to take a stand against Goliath. Let's look at a few verses:

> 32And David said to Saul, "Let no man's heart fail because of him. Your servant will go and fight with this Philistine."
> 33 And Saul said to David, "You are not able to go against this Philistine to fight with him, for you are but a youth, and he has been a man of war from his youth." 37 And David said, "The Lord who delivered me from the paw of the lion and from the paw of the bear will deliver me from the hand of this Philistine." And Saul said to David, "Go, and the Lord be with you!"

> 1 Samuel 17:32-33, 37 (ESV)

While the whole army of Israel was afraid of Goliath, David wasn't. Why? It's not because David trusted in his own ability, or his own strength. Rather, he trusted in God. He wasn't concerned with how big Goliath was, or how mighty Goliath was. David knew how big God was. He knew how mighty and powerful God was. He knew that God could do anything.

All throughout the Bible, we see God move mightily, we see God do the miraculous. Specifically, we see Him flood the entire Earth, split the Red Sea, rain down bread from Heaven, heal all kinds of diseases, and even bring the dead back to life. He does what no one else can do.

Nothing is impossible for God. God can do anything.

ASK FOR A MIRACLE

No matter how big our problems are, God is always bigger. No matter how impossible the situation may seem, nothing is impossible for God. So, let's be intentional about asking God to do what only He can do. Ask God to move in your situation. Ask God to do the impossible. Ask God for a miracle.

I hope you never have to face a financial hardship, but if you ever do:

- Maybe you lose your job.

- Maybe you're backed up on your rent.

- Maybe you have no money for food, bills, or rent.

I remember there was a time in my life when I was down and out financially. My wife and I were without jobs, without cars, and without a home of our own. It seemed like no matter what we did, we couldn't get out of the rut we were in. But one day, during the holidays, a woman came to our church and gave us a Christmas card. Inside that card was $2,000. That money helped us get a car, and it was a turning point for us getting out of our financial struggles in that season. This woman didn't really know what our situation was, but God did. And God moved through this woman to intervene in our situation, and help us through. The same God who helped me can help you as well.

Ask for a miracle. Remind yourself that God can do anything. He is bigger than the situation. Have faith that God can help you.

> **24** Therefore I tell you, whatever you ask for in prayer, believe that you have received it, and it will be yours.

> Mark 11:24 (NIV)

I hope you never have to suffer through health problems, but if you ever do:

- Maybe you're in constant pain.

- Maybe you've been diagnosed with a life-threatening condition.

- Maybe the doctors say your situation is impossible.

Ask for a miracle. Ask God to heal you. Remind yourself that God can do anything. Again, He is bigger than the situation. Have faith that God is able to make you well.

There was a time at a Bible Study that a woman asked for prayer regarding her hip. Her hip was out of alignment, and causing a whole lot of pain for her. In fact, she had a hard time sleeping because of it. It turns out that she was already seeing a doctor about it, and discussing the option of surgery. Those of us at the Bible Study prayed for her that night, believing that God can do anything. The very next week, this woman came back wanting to share an update. She had seen her doctor that week, and the doctor basically said, "I don't know why we have another order for an X-ray, we already did X-rays, but let's get some more." When the X-rays came back, the doctor pulled her in and said, "I don't know what happened. As you can see, these are your old X-rays, and you can clearly see the alignment issue. But here are the new X-rays, and it's showing that there's nothing wrong."

No one can tell me that God doesn't do miracles. No one can tell me that miracles don't happen anymore. I've seen God move. I've seen God heal different kinds of pain and health conditions. There's no doubt in my mind that God can do anything.

There's absolutely no problem, no pain, no sickness, and no disease, that is too much for our God to handle. There's no mountain that's too big for God to move. There's no situation too permanent for God to intervene. Nothing is impossible for God. God can do anything. Believe that. Trust that. Have faith in that. And demonstrate that faith by asking God for a miracle.

YOU CAN HAVE HOPE

Imagine what it would be like if we were absolutely convinced that God can do anything. Think about how much more peace we would have. Think about how much more joy and contentment we would have, even in the midst of hard times. Just imagine the testimony it would be to our family and friends to see us in such high spirits, even when we're going through the fire. No fear, no anxiety, just faith, hope, and trust in a God that can do anything.

Imagine the miracles we'll open ourselves up to seeing God do in our lives. Just hang on to this truth: God can do anything.

CHALLENGE

I want to challenge you this week to take a step forward in trusting that God can do anything. Sometimes, problems can be so overwhelming that we can't see past them. In those moments, it's not always that we don't believe that God can do anything. We just need to be reminded about it. This challenge will help you keep that front and center, so that when hard times come your way, it will be second nature to remind yourself that God can do anything.

Every day this week, I want to challenge you to spend a moment observing God's creation. That could mean observing the night sky, or standing on a beach, or looking towards some mountains, or whatever is appropriate for where you live. As you observe God's creation, tell God, "If You can speak this into existence, You can do anything in my life."

GOD LOVES US NO MATTER WHAT

Have you ever let somebody down?

I remember when my son, Micah, was about 3 years old, we went on a spontaneous Disneyland trip. At the time, we had Disneyland passes, and we were super excited to go spend the evening at Disneyland. When we got there, the lines for the gate were pretty short, which is always a good sign. So, we get up to the gate, they scan our passes, and the cast member says, "Oh wait, I'm sorry, but your passes are blocked-out today." Micah didn't quite catch it when the cast member told us, he was already walking into the park. We had to tell him, "Wait! Micah, come back." Then we had to go inside to get him, and take him out of the park. And I remember clear as day, kneeling down and telling him, "I'm so sorry, we can't go inside the park today. I should have checked to see if our passes were good today, and I didn't." As I'm telling him, he is crying. It wasn't a bratty cry, but a genuine sad cry.

Man, that was hard, that broke my heart. I felt so bad. I felt like I had let him down.

The reality is many of us have disappointed someone we love, whether it be our parents, our spouse, our children, our boss, or someone else. When we do that, it makes us feel like failures, it makes us feel like we're not wanted, like we aren't worthy, like we don't deserve to be loved. Honestly, it can make us feel like we don't want to show our face.

Unfortunately, we carry over a lot of these feelings into Christianity. When we disobey God, it's easy to feel like we are disappointing Him, and letting Him down. This generally leads to feelings of shame and guilt. On top of that, as soon as we mess up, the enemy is right there telling us that we're a failure, that we don't deserve God's love. He'll tell us God is upset with us, that we've blown it for the last time, that there are no more chances, and that we're hypocrites. These are ugly thoughts and ugly feelings.

I wish we never had to go through times like that. However, the truth is, we are going to mess up. We are still a work in progress, and there will be times that we disobey God, or fall short. So, the question is, how are we supposed to handle these situations? How do we prevent ourselves from being swallowed up by guilt and shame? Fortunately for us, the Bible teaches a truth about God that has the power to transform the way we see God, ourselves, and our shortcomings. We can be free from the shackles of shame, guilt, and the lies of the enemy.

JOHN 3:16-17

The passage of scripture we're going to focus on is John 3:16-17. Let's take a look:

> 16 "For God so loved the world, that he gave his only Son, that whoever believes in him should not perish but have eternal life. 17 For God did not

send his Son into the world to condemn the world, but in order that the world might be saved through him.

John 3:16-17 (ESV)

What a shock these words might have been to some. I mean, sure, we know God loved His chosen people, the Jewish people. But Jesus doesn't just mention the Jews. He says, God loved the world, the whole world. That means every single person, of every nation, of every color, of every religion. And it's not just a general love for His creation, but rather, it is an individual, specific, and personal love for each human being. God's love is so far-reaching, it's beyond our comprehension.

His love wasn't just in words either, but God demonstrated it with action. Not just any action, but the greatest act of selflessness and sacrifice the world has ever seen.

Because God loves us, He wants what is best for us, and ultimately, that is eternal life. But there's a problem: each one of us has sinned against God. In other words, we have all disobeyed God in one way or another. The Bible says that the punishment for acts of disobedience is death, meaning spiritual death as well as physical death. And that's just for one act of disobedience. I don't know about you, but I've disobeyed God more than one time. As a result of all our sin, we have accrued for ourselves a massive punishment. It's like a debt that we cannot pay. If we think about it in terms of a prison sentence, it's like receiving 5,000 life sentences in prison. There's no way we'd ever be able to serve the full sentence.

There's an even deeper issue though, beyond our individual acts of sin. The Bible says that the first people ever created were Adam and Eve. In Genesis, we can read about the very first time they sinned and rebelled against God's commands. When that happened, sin entered the world, and because of their sin, we've all been born with a nature to sin. By nature, our spirit is dead, and our hearts are wicked. Our natural inclination is to sin, to disobey God. It's our nature now. So, we are not sinners because we have committed single acts of sin. Rather, we commit acts of sin because deep inside we are sinners.

As we touched on earlier, God loves us and wants us to have eternal life. He wants us to go to Heaven. However, our sinful nature coupled with our acts of disobedience have put a giant wedge in the way. There's literally no possible way we could be good enough to deserve eternal life, to deserve Heaven. We rightfully deserve the wrath and judgment of God.

The only way to Heaven for us, or anyone else, was to offer a substitute to pay the death penalty that we deserve. This is where God stepped in to demonstrate His great love for us. Who was pure enough, holy enough, perfect enough, to take our place as a substitute? Only Jesus, God's perfect Son. Only through the death and resurrection of Jesus could we inherit eternal life. Only Jesus could pay our debt. Only He can take on the death penalty that we deserve. Only He can embrace the wrath and judgment of God that is rightfully ours. No one else could have done this, it had to be the Son of God. Only Jesus could be the ultimate sacrifice, the ultimate substitute, the ultimate Lamb of God, providing a way for the forgiveness of all sins, past, present, and future. So, because of God's great love for us, He did the unthinkable, so that we can inherit eternal life. He sacrificed His only Son.

I wonder, do you happen to have any children?

I'm going to tell you something, I love my kids. Like, seriously, I love my kids. I would do absolutely anything for my kids. I never ever want to see them hurt.

A couple of years ago, on Father's Day, my family was out eating ice cream at Cold Stone Creamery in Lakewood, CA. We were sitting outside, just hanging out and talking. And suddenly, my oldest son, Micah, fell and hit the back of his head on a concrete curb. The back of his head was cut open, maybe about a quarter size in diameter, and about an inch deep. I remember my mother-in-law, Nancy, was putting pressure on it, and blood was just pouring out like a faucet. We got him in the car and rushed him to the ER. I'll tell you, at that moment, I didn't care about anyone or anything else. My son was hurt, and all I could think about was getting him treatment as fast as I could. I didn't care about the speed limit, I didn't care about the rules of the road. I was driving on the opposite side of the road, going as fast as I could. Luckily, a cop didn't try to pull us over. But I honestly think if a cop came up behind me, I wouldn't have stopped.

I can't for one second imagine willingly sacrificing my son for someone else. Don't get me wrong, I love people, but I'm not sure I'm willing to put my son's life in danger for it. Yet, God sacrificed His one and only Son to make a way for you and I to know Him and to be with Him for all eternity. How amazing is that?

> [13] The greatest love people can show is to die for their friends.

> John 15:13 (ERV)

We're not done yet. You see, God didn't just make the ultimate sacrifice, He made it for people who were His enemies. It's one thing to sacrifice for someone who loves you. But it's a whole other thing to sacrifice for someone who hates you.

> [6] For while we were still weak, at the right time Christ died for the ungodly. [7] For one will scarcely die for a righteous person—though perhaps

for a good person one would dare even to die— **8** but God shows his love for us in that while we were still sinners, Christ died for us.

Romans 5:6-8 (ESV)

God didn't sacrifice Jesus for a worthy people. He didn't sacrifice His Son for people who deserved such a sacrifice. God sacrificed His only Son for messed up, broken, and sinful people who willingly lived in rebellion against Him. There's not one single person who deserves this kind of sacrifice. There's not one single person who deserves this kind of love.

We were dead in our trespasses and sins. We were enemies of God. And yet, God still loved us. That still blows my mind. He could have just started over with creation. He could have just decided to wipe everyone and everything out, and just start over again. But He didn't. Why? Because He loves us.

8 … God is love.

1 John 4:8 (ESV)

Love is in His nature. It's who He is. God loves us, and He will always love us.

GOD LOVES US NO MATTER WHAT

God loves us no matter what. This is good news because it means that God's love is not based on us. It's not based on how good we are, how holy we are, or how righteous we are. It's not even based on whether or not we are willing to accept it. It's an unconditional love.

Maybe you don't feel lovable. God's love for you goes way behind what you do, what you offer, or even how good you think you are. I understand that this is sometimes hard for us to comprehend, because as humans, it's easy to love someone or something because of what they do for us, or how they make us feel. But God's love is bigger than that.

God can see the depths of our souls, and the intentions of our hearts. He can see right past any mask we wear. He knows the true us, however wicked or pure, and yet, He still loves us. We don't have to pretend to be something we are not. We do not have to meet a certain standard. God still loves us. We don't have to earn that. In fact, we can't earn it, even if we tried. It's freely available, with no conditions.

If God loved us when we were His enemies, when we were dead in our trespasses and sins, then there's nothing we could ever do to make Him love us any less. God loves us no matter what.

> **38-39** Yes, I am sure that nothing can separate us from God's love—not death, life, angels, or ruling spirits. I am sure that nothing now, nothing in the future, no powers, nothing above us or nothing below us—nothing in the whole created world—will ever be able to separate us from the love God has shown us in Christ Jesus our Lord.
>
> Romans 8:38-39 (ERV)

REBUKE THE LIES

Unfortunately, we often act, live, and feel like God's love is dependent upon what we do. When we mess up, we often feel unworthy of

God's love and acceptance. We are too ashamed to pray and draw close to God. Can I tell you something? This is exactly what the devil wants. The devil will try to keep you from drawing near to God. He is going to try to tell you that you are unworthy, that you don't deserve to come before God. He is going to try to fill your mind and heart with condemnation, shame, and guilt. Don't allow it. Rebuke the lies. If we allow condemnation and shame to overwhelm us and keep us from drawing close to God, only the enemy wins. It does us no good. We don't have to feel that way. God loves us no matter what.

Maybe you're facing a situation like this right now. Maybe you've done some things you're not proud of. Maybe you've made some mistakes. Maybe you've made a promise to God to never engage in a particular sin again, and then you ended up failing to keep that promise. I want you to know, not only have I been there, but some of the people God used most mightily in the Bible experienced times like that as well. David, for instance, was called a man after God's own heart, and he committed adultery and murder. Abraham, who was given the tremendous promise that all nations of the world would be blessed through him, straight up lied to people out of fear. Peter, who walked with Jesus, who had seen so many mighty miracles and heard such great teaching from Jesus, denied that he even knew Him.

People make mistakes. People fall short. That's not an excuse to sin. God most definitely wants us to be free from all sin, and the Holy Spirit is constantly working in our hearts to sanctify us. But even in our shortcomings, God still loves us. Your intimacy with God may vary, but no matter how far God feels to you, you can always know that He loves you.

Never let Satan, or anyone else, convince you that God doesn't love you anymore. Listen, God doesn't hate you. No matter what you've done, God is ready to forgive. God is ready to receive us. God is willing to hear us. God will not turn us away. When we fall short, we can boldly, and confidently, enter into God's presence, seeking forgiveness, healing, and restoration.

> ¹⁶ Let us then approach God's throne of grace with confidence, so that we may

receive mercy and find grace to help us in our time of need.

Hebrews 4:16 (NIV)

YOU ARE LOVED

When we sin, when we fall short, and when we deal with moral failures, we can respond with feelings of shame and guilt. We can allow shame and guilt to make us feel like God doesn't want us, or like God doesn't love us. We can allow ourselves to be convinced that we don't deserve God's love. We can choose to stay away from God. We can choose to stay away from God's people.

That's not the life I want to live. And I dare say that it's not what you want either. You may not be, or feel, loved by very many people in this world, but you are loved by the creator of the universe. You never, ever, ever, ever have to question whether God loves you. God loves you no matter what.

CHALLENGE

I want to challenge you for the next week to take a small step forward in embracing the truth that God loves us no matter what.

For the next week, spend a few moments each day remembering who you were before Jesus. Think about the kinds of sins you were involved in, the type of character you had, and the deep heart issues. As you recall these things, spend some time thanking God that He loved you even then.

GOD IS ALWAYS WITH US

> ## HAS THERE EVER BEEN
> ## A TIME IN YOUR LIFE WHEN
> ## YOU FELT ALONE?

Has there ever been a time in your life when you felt alone?

When I was about five years old, my sister and I were placed in California's foster care system. I remember not understanding what was going on, or where I was. Literally, a man picked me up from my dad's house, and I was dropped off at a stranger's house. On top of that, my sister was placed in a different home than I was. To this day, I can vividly remember wondering where my sister was, hoping to see her. I don't think I ever felt so alone.

Maybe you've been through some situations that made you feel like that. Maybe you've been through some things that made you feel alone or abandoned.

If we're honest, there are times in life when it's easy to feel alone, like:

- When we lose a loved one.

- When a relationship is ended.

- When we go through a hard time, and no one is there to help us.

Unfortunately, as long as we're here on this earth, there will likely be times when it feels like no one is there to help us, to support us, or to encourage us. There will likely be times when people we love are no longer around. There will likely be times we will be betrayed, left out, rejected, neglected, or forgotten.

People all over this world are going through situations at this very moment that are making them feel like:

- No one cares about them.

- No one notices them.

- No one sees their pain.

- No one hears them.

Perhaps it's a rumor that's going around. Maybe it's some kind of abuse behind closed doors that no one knows about. Perhaps it's someone feeling they don't fit in at school, or at work, or at church. Maybe it's a bully making fun of someone, making them feel insignificant and rejected.

Truthfully, even as a Christian, we can sometimes experience these things. Even in our relationship with God, we can sometimes experience these things. There are times we can wonder, "God, where are you?"

These are ugly feelings, and they can lead to things like depression and even suicidal thoughts.

The good news is that the Bible addresses this. In fact, the Bible shows us examples of people who felt this exact way. So, let's take a look at a particular passage of scripture in Daniel 3, and we're going to talk about a central truth about

God that will radically transform the way we deal with these kinds of problems.

DANIEL 3:19-25

As a bit of background information, three men (Shadrach, Meshach, and Abednego) refused to worship a golden statue that Nebuchadnezzar, the king of Babylon, had set up. So, the king of Babylon tells them that he is going to put them in a fiery furnace to be burned alive. In fact, the king orders the furnace to be turned up seven times hotter than usual.

If there was ever a time to feel alone, this was it. If there was ever a time to feel abandoned by God, this was it. If there was ever a time to question God's presence, this was it. Imagine what could be going on in the minds of Shadrach, Meshach, and Abednego. Here they are doing the right thing, obeying God. Yet, it seems like God has abandoned them. They are about to be burned to death in a furnace, and it seems like God is nowhere to be found. It would have been easy for them to think, "God, where are you?"

When these three men end up getting thrown into the furnace, something crazy happens. Let's read it.

19 Then Nebuchadnezzar became very angry with Shadrach, Meshach, and Abednego. He gave an order for the oven to be heated seven times hotter than it usually was. **20** Then he commanded some of the strongest soldiers in his army to tie up Shadrach, Meshach, and Abednego. He told the soldiers to throw them into the hot furnace.

21 So Shadrach, Meshach, and Abednego were tied up and thrown into the hot furnace. They were wearing their robes, pants, cloth caps, and other clothes. **22** The king was very angry when he gave the command, so the soldiers quickly made the furnace very hot. The fire was so hot that the flames killed the strong soldiers. They were killed when they went close to the fire to throw in Shadrach, Meshach, and Abednego. **23** Shadrach, Meshach, and Abednego fell into the fire. They were tied up very tightly.

24 Then King Nebuchadnezzar jumped to his feet. He was very surprised and he asked his advisors, "We tied only three men, and we threw only three men into the fire. Is that right?"

His advisors said, "Yes, King."

25 The king said, "Look! I see four men walking around in the fire. They are not tied up and they are not burned. The fourth man looks like an angel."

Daniel 3:19-25 (ERV)

On the outside, it might have looked like these men were alone. It might have seemed like God had abandoned them. But the truth is, God didn't leave them. God didn't abandon them. God was always there with them. In fact, God was even with them in the fire! Rest assured, God will be with you in the fire as well.

GOD IS ALWAYS WITH US

God is always with us.

Just as God was there with Shadrach, Meshach, and Abednego, God is here with us as well. As a follower of Jesus, wherever you're at, whatever you're going through, you can know that God is always with you.

God is not just some distant being sitting in Heaven somewhere, merely looking down on all of us. God is omnipresent. He can be anywhere at any time. He is not limited to being in one place at a time.

> 7 Where can I go from your Spirit?
>
> Where can I flee from your presence?
>
> 8 If I go up to the heavens, you are there;
>
> if I make my bed in the depths, you are there.

Psalm 139:7-8 (NIV)

There is not a single place where God is not present. Not only that, but God is also fully present in every place as well. He is not divided.

He is not partially here, and partially there. He is fully here and fully there; He is fully everywhere.

Now, He doesn't always manifest Himself in easily visible ways, as we see occasionally in the Bible. For example, in Exodus, we see God manifest His presence in the form of a burning bush, a pillar of cloud, and a pillar of fire. Nevertheless, He is still ever-present.

God is always with us, whether we believe it or not, whether we see it or not, and whether we like it or not. That means, He knows what we're going through. That means, He hears us. We are known, we are seen, we are heard. We don't have to go through things alone.

> [1] God is our refuge and strength,
>
> a very present help in trouble.
>
> Psalm 46:1 (ESV)

Isn't that amazing? There are over 6 billion people on this planet, but God still knows you, He still knows me, and He is still present with us in every moment. We don't have to call and make an appointment. We don't have to schedule a meeting. We don't have to spend 4 hours in prayer or worship for Him to be with us. Right where you're at you can enjoy the full presence of God at the exact same moment people in Germany, Egypt, or Hong Kong, are experiencing the full presence of God.

It's important to understand though, that just because God is present, that doesn't mean all of life will be smooth sailing. I think we sometimes feel that if God is with us, we won't experience any difficult situations. There's a story in the Bible, from John 11, that reminds me of this mindset. In John 11, a man named Lazarus dies, and Jesus goes to visit the family a few days later. Here is what Lazarus' sister, Martha, says to Jesus:

> 21 Martha then said to Jesus, "Lord, if You had been here, my brother would not have died.

> John 11:21 (NASB)

Have you ever felt like that? These kinds of thoughts manifest in several ways, like:

- "If You were here, I wouldn't be going through this!"

- "If You were here, my child wouldn't be suffering!"

- "If You were here, I wouldn't be feeling like this!"

God certainly can help in our situations. He is able to heal, to restore, and to rescue. We see this with Shadrach, Meshach, and Abednego, where God was with them and protected them in the fire. But whether God protected them or not, He was still going to be with them. The same is true for us. There are times God will protect us from messed up situations, and there are times when God will simply walk with us through those difficult circumstances. Either way, He is with us.

ACKNOWLEDGE IT

If God is always with us, then that means you are never alone. Listen, you are not alone. I am not alone. The whole world might leave us. Our friends and family might abandon us.

Nevertheless, God is always with us, and He promises to never leave us or forsake us.

> [5] "I will never leave you nor forsake you."

Hebrews 13:5 (ESV)

People we love dearly, including our friends, family members, our spouses, and our children, might leave us. They might walk away from us. They might abandon us. People we thought would always be there can sometimes turn their back on us. However, God will never do that.

We don't have to face life alone. We don't have to go through the fire alone. We have a friend who is always near. We have the best friend, the best counselor, the best teacher, and the best comforter, with us all day.

When a loved one dies, we don't have to feel alone. When we're facing a hard time, we don't have to feel like no one cares, or no one understands. God is always with us.

We can lean on Him.

We can talk to Him.

We can trust Him.

We can rely on Him.

We can seek His advice.

We can seek His help.

That means, we can pray to God anytime, anywhere. Regardless of what's going on or where we're at, we can talk with God. Even if we don't feel like talking, we can just be with God. We can just sit with God if we want to, and let Him speak to us, or comfort us. The bottom line is, He's there. We just need to acknowledge it.

YOU ARE NOT ALONE

Imagine what it would be like to live every moment of our lives knowing without a shadow of a doubt that God was right there next to us, through the thick and thin. Just imagine how much more confidence we would have when facing tough situations, or how much more faith we would have for God to move. It would be like having our big brother behind us when some schoolyard bullies try to mess with us.

Imagine never feeling alone, never feeling abandoned, never feeling like no one knows. We can live this way if we hang on to this one truth: God is always with us.

CHALLENGE

I want to challenge you this week to take a step forward in walking out this truth. The goal of this challenge is to become more aware of His presence. You see, the question is never whether God is with us or not. Rather, the question is are we aware of His presence.

One way we can be reminded of God's presence is in the way we pray. So often, we pray like God is somewhere distant. We pray to God like He is far away, in the heavens somewhere. For sure, He is. But He is also right there with us. So, for the next week, I want to challenge you to pray like God is right next to you.

Think about it this way, treat God as if He was your best friend. Imagine that you spent the entire day, from the moment you woke up, to the moment you fell asleep, with your best friend by your side. What would you do? Would you talk to them? How much would you talk to them? This week, think of God as right there with you, and talk with Him throughout the day – about anything and everything. By the end of the week, I guarantee you'll feel closer to God, and you'll be more aware of His presence in your life.

GOD IS IN CONTROL

> **WHEN'S THE LAST TIME YOU FACED A PROBLEM THAT YOU DIDN'T HAVE THE POWER TO FIX?**

When's the last time you faced a problem that you didn't have the power to fix?

On February 3, 2021, my family was hit by one of the most difficult times we had ever faced. Late December 2020 to mid-January 2021, our entire household became infected with COVID-19. That alone was a battle, but by late January, we had all recovered, and felt very grateful for that. Then, out of nowhere, we noticed that my son, Micah, started having fevers every day, and his body began to swell up. When February 3rd came around, Micah was taken to Urgent Care. We expected them to prescribe him some medicine and send him home. Instead, Urgent Care recommended that we take him to a Children's Hospital. So, my wife took him to the

ER at a Children's Hospital nearby. Again, we expected the hospital to simply send him home with some prescriptions. As soon as Micah was seen by the ER, everything escalated very quickly. What we thought was going to be a quick visit to get some good medicine, turned into an 11-day stay where we weren't certain that Micah was going to make it out alive.

Micah was diagnosed with MIS-C, which seems to be related to COVID-19 in children. He suffered from severe inflammation, incredible stomach pain, migraine headaches, rashes all over his body, an uncontrollable fever, diarrhea, and more. He could hardly talk, and he couldn't handle any noise or light in the room.

It was so hard to see my child that sick. It felt like there was nothing I could do. I couldn't give him medicine to make him feel better. I couldn't cuddle with him, because every time I touched him, it would hurt him. It felt like there was nothing I could physically do to make this situation better.

What do you do in times like these?

Perhaps you've been through situations like this. Maybe you're even going through something like this right now.

What do you do when ...

- you've been diagnosed with a rare disease that has no cure?

- you're struggling with infertility, or wrestling with the pain of a miscarriage?

- you're a victim of abuse?

- the economy goes south and leaves you without a job?

- your spouse decides they want out of the marriage?

- you're hit by another driver on the road?

- a loved one is on their death bed?

What are we supposed to do when the situation is outside of our control? What are we supposed to do when there's nothing we can do to fix the problem?

Let's be honest, there are times we face issues that have some real practical solutions. In other words, sometimes there are things we can do in the physical realm to resolve some of the problems we face. However, there are also times we face things beyond our control. I'm talking about times when there's absolutely nothing we could have done to prevent the situation, and it feels like there's nothing we could do to resolve it either.

The truth is, things are going to happen that are simply outside of our control. If you've ever gone through these types of situations, you know it's easy to feel stressed out, overwhelmed, hopeless, powerless, like there's nothing we can do. So, what do you do in those situations? How are we supposed to respond? How are we supposed to cope?

The Bible offers a truth about God that will help us navigate these situations and respond to these kinds of problems in a much different way. We can see this truth illustrated very clearly in Job 1:6-12.

JOB 1:6-12

As a bit of context, the first chapter of Job opens up by introducing us to a man named Job. He was a God-fearing man who lived a tremendously blessed and prosperous life. Verse 6 picks up on a day when everything was about to change for Job. Let's read Job 1:6-12.

> **6-7** One day when the angels came to report to God, Satan, who was the Designated Accuser, came along with them. God singled out Satan and said, "What have you been up to?"
>
> Satan answered God, "Going here and there, checking things out on earth."
>
> **8** God said to Satan, "Have you noticed my friend Job? There's no one quite like him—honest and true to his word, totally devoted to God and hating evil."
>
> **9-10** Satan retorted, "So do you think Job does all that out of the sheer goodness of his heart? Why, no one ever had it so good! You pamper him like a pet, make sure nothing bad ever happens

to him or his family or his possessions, bless everything he does—he can't lose!

[11] "But what do you think would happen if you reached down and took away everything that is his? He'd curse you right to your face, that's what."

[12] God replied, "We'll see. Go ahead— do what you want with all that is his. Just don't hurt *him*." Then Satan left the presence of God.

Job 1:6-12 (MSG)

The rest of Job 1 details what happens next. In one tragic day, Job essentially loses everything. He loses his animals. He loses his servants. Then, as if things couldn't get any worse, his children were killed. All this in one day.

Imagine how hopeless Job must have felt. Imagine how powerless Job must have felt. Imagine how overwhelmed Job must have felt. Imagine the questions that must have been going through his mind.

What I want to point out, though, is that Satan needed permission from God to do what he did. In fact, we see that God even restricts Satan from harming Job's physical body. In Job 2, Satan comes before God again, and God gives the devil permission to afflict Job's body, as long as he doesn't kill Job.

We must understand that Satan is not God's equal. As much damage as the devil does in this world, and as much corruption as he causes, he cannot do something that God doesn't allow. God is the ultimate power.

Everything that happens is either commanded by God or allowed by God. He is sovereign over all things. He is in control of all things. He has the final say.

GOD IS IN CONTROL

God is in control. In fact, there's not a single thing that God is not in control of.

We even see this demonstrated in the life and ministry of Jesus.

23 And when he got into the boat, his disciples followed him. **24** And behold, there arose a great storm on the sea, so that the boat was being swamped by the waves; but he was asleep. **25** And they went and woke him, saying, "Save us, Lord; we are perishing." **26** And he said to them, "Why are you afraid, O you of little faith?" Then he rose and rebuked the winds and the sea, and there was a great calm. **27** And the men marveled, saying, "What sort of man is this, that even winds and sea obey him?"

Matthew 8:23-27 (ESV)

Maybe you've told another person what to do, but have you ever tried to tell the weather what to do? Jesus simply speaks to the wind and the sea, and they obey Him. This is more than just power. This is absolute control. This is supreme authority. This is sovereignty. This is lordship. This is kingship.

All throughout the Bible, we see God demonstrate control over the weather, animals, sicknesses, diseases, evil spirits, and even events. At His command, all sickness must leave the body. At His command, all evil spirits must flee.

> 27 And they were all amazed, so that they questioned among themselves, saying, "What is this? A new teaching with authority! He commands even the unclean spirits, and they obey him."

Mark 1:27 (ESV)

He is the creator of all things. He's the sustainer of all things. Without Him, there would be no earth. Without Him, there would be no mankind. Without Him, there would be no space, time, or matter.

> 17 He existed before anything else,
>
> and he holds all creation together.

Colossians 1:17 (NLT)

All throughout the history of the world, and the history of our lives, there's never been a time that God was not in control. That's good news, because even when things seem out of control, I can trust that God is still in control. Even when I feel my situation is beyond my control, I can trust that God is definitely still in control.

Being completely transparent, when we're facing a hard time, it can be hard to see how God is in control. It doesn't always make sense why God would allow certain things to happen. Realistically, some of us will face trials and situations that are absolutely horrendous. Some of us will face things that we feel no one should ever have to deal with. Yet, even in those times, we must understand that God is ultimately in control. The good news is that He has the final say, and He can take the most terrible situation and turn it around for good.

> **28** And we know that God causes everything to work together for the good of those who love God and are called according to his purpose for them.
>
> Romans 8:28 (NLT)

Who knows, maybe God is planning to use our bad situation for good, or for His glory. I know it can be hard to understand how God can use something like a miscarriage, or child abuse, to bring about good, but He does. Maybe God wants to draw us closer to Him, or maybe He wants to grow us through the situation. Perhaps God wants us to be able to comfort others who go through similar circumstances. No matter what, though, we can trust that God is in control. The same God who loves us, hears us, and has a plan for our lives, is the same God who is in control of our situation.

GO TO GOD FIRST

Ultimately, if we believe that God is in control, then whenever we come face to face with a trial, a problem, or a difficult circumstance in our lives, the very first thing we should do is go to God in prayer.

That means going to God before trying to fix things ourselves. Before trying to make things right by our own strength, our own power, or our own ability, we should go to God first. After all, He's the One who has ultimate authority and control over every situation.

Not so long ago, my wife, Cynthia, left by herself to run an errand. I was in my room working,

Micah was in his room, and our youngest son, Ezra, who was two years old at the time, was in the living room watching TV.

While Cynthia was driving, she had a vision of Ezra walking out of the house by himself and getting hit by a black truck. At this point, she realized her phone was dead, and she was miles away.

Now, she could have rushed back like a crazy woman, speeding and swerving all the way home. She could have freaked out and panicked. And if we're honest, that's how many of us would react naturally. Cynthia had all the reason in the world to feel hopeless and powerless.

That's not how Cynthia reacted though, because she 100% believes that God is in control of everything. So, she went straight to God, and said, "God, please protect Ezra."

Around the same time, I got a weird feeling, so I went to check on Ezra. Low and behold, the front door was wide open, and a neighbor was walking Ezra back to our house. Apparently, Ezra opened both the locked front door, and the locked screen door by himself, and ran outside yelling, "Mommy!"

There's nothing Cynthia could have done in that situation, except pray, and trust that God is in control. That's the key to having real peace in these situations. We need to go to God first.

YOU CAN HAVE PEACE

When we're hit by a situation that is beyond our control, we can respond by allowing ourselves to feel hopeless and powerless. We can allow ourselves to be stressed out. We can allow ourselves to be overwhelmed and frustrated.

But it doesn't have to be that way. We can respond differently. We can live our lives never having to feel hopeless. We can live our lives never having to feel powerless. We can live our lives never having to be stressed out and overwhelmed by our problems. We can experience peace, real peace. The key is trusting that God is in control of everything.

The God who is in control of everything is the same God who loves me, died for me, and wants what is absolutely best for me.

CHALLENGE

I want to challenge you this week to take a step forward in trusting that God is in control. This challenge is aimed at aligning your heart and your mind with this truth each day.

For the next week, at the start of each day, I want to challenge you to spend a moment with God in prayer, and say, "God, no matter what happens today, I trust that You are in control."

A PREREQUISITE FOR PEACE

It's entirely possible that you read through this entire book, and yet, you are not an active follower of Jesus. If that's you, I want you to know that the peace that's talked about in this book can be yours. However, it requires a big decision, perhaps the biggest decision you'll ever make in your life. The first step in experiencing peace, the kind of peace we've talked about in the previous chapters, is confessing Jesus as Lord and Savior.

> 9 If you declare with your mouth, "Jesus is Lord," and believe in your heart that God raised him from the dead, you will be saved.
>
> Romans 10:9 (NIV)

What does that mean? What does that entail? Allow me to explain.

You see, there is a real God who really created all things. He loves us, He has a plan and purpose for us. His desire is that we know Him, love Him, and spend all eternity with Him. However, we have separated ourselves from Him because, one way or another, we have all disobeyed Him. This is called sin.

The thing is, God is holy, perfect, and just. He can have nothing to do with sin. In fact, He has ordained that the punishment for disobeying Him is death. So, because of our disobedience, we are all spiritually dead, and separated from God. We are all on a path to judgment and God's wrath. Basically, we're headed for hell.

The good news is, the Bible says that God loved the world so much that He sent His only Son, Jesus, to come live a perfect, sinless life, and sacrifice His own life for the sins of the world. Essentially, He paid the death penalty that we deserve. He took on the judgment and wrath of God that we deserve.

And now, the Bible says, if we put our faith in Jesus, if we confess Jesus as Lord and Savior, and believe that God raised Him from the dead, we will be saved. Confessing Him as Lord means acknowledging Him as our master, or boss. If Jesus is our Lord, we do what He says. To confess Jesus as Savior is to admit He is the only one who can save us from sin and death. So, if we confess Jesus as Lord and Savior, and believe that God raised Him from the dead, we will be saved. Saved from what? Saved from the punishment of sin. We'll be saved from the wrath of God. We'll be saved from the death penalty that we deserve.

The moment we put our faith in Jesus, everything changes. At that moment, all of our sins from the past, the present, and the future, are forgiven. Instantaneously. At that moment, we are declared holy, not because of what we've done, but because of what Jesus has done for us. At that moment, we are made right with God, no longer separated from Him. That means we get to have a relationship with God. We get to know God in a real and personal way. Isn't that amazing? We get direct access to God Almighty, the creator of the universe. He no longer looks at us as messed up sinners. He doesn't just see us as liars, or thieves, or addicts, or murderers, or sinful people. He sees us as holy children of God. And for the rest of our lives, we have the Holy Spirit dwelling in us, helping us to be all that God's called us to be. Not only that, but we inherit the promise of eternal life with God in Heaven.

This could be your moment. If you want to put your faith in Jesus as Lord and Savior, and be forgiven for all of your sins, I'm going to ask you to repeat the following prayer to God:

> Heavenly Father,
>
> I confess Jesus Christ as Lord and Savior.
>
> I believe in my heart that You raised Him from the dead.
>
> Please, forgive me for all my sins.
>
> I repent.
>
> Please, fill me with Your Holy Spirit.
>
> Help me to live for You from this day forward.
>
> In Jesus' name I pray, amen.

If you just repeated that prayer, and you meant it from your heart, you just made the best decision in your life. But, don't stop there. I encourage you to take a few next steps:

1. Find, visit, and join a local church. If you have friends or relatives already attending a church, consider checking those out first.

2. Devote some time each day to read the Bible. If this is your first time, the Gospel of John is a good place to start.

3. Spend a few moments each day praying to God. Talk to Him about anything and everything.

God has a plan and a purpose for your life. May you experience it to the fullest.

CONCLUSION

You and I can have peace through every problem.

There's peace knowing that even when the situation seems impossible, GOD CAN DO ANYTHING.

There's peace knowing that even when we fall short, GOD LOVES US NO MATTER WHAT.

There's peace knowing that even when we feel alone, GOD IS ALWAYS WITH US.

There's peace knowing that even when there's nothing we can do, GOD IS IN CONTROL.

May the four simple truths that we unpacked in this book forever transform the way we think about our circumstances, the way we react to problems, and even the way we interact with God through prayer. Forevermore, when we pray, may we always:

- Pray with faith, knowing that God can do anything.

- Pray with confidence, knowing that God loves us no matter what.

- Pray like God is next to us, knowing that He is always with us.

- Pray before we do anything else, knowing that God is in control.

  [6] Don't worry about anything; instead, pray about everything. Tell God what you need, and thank him for all he has done. [7] Then you will experience God's peace, which exceeds anything we can understand. His peace will guard your hearts and minds as you live in Christ Jesus.

  Philippians 4:6-7 (NLT)